Bread Without Sugar

ALSO BY GERALD STERN

Leaving Another Kingdom: Selected Poems

Two Long Poems

Lovesick

Paradise Poems

The Red Coal

Lucky Life

Rejoicings

Bread Without Sugar

P o e m s

Gerald Stern

W·W·Norton & Company   *New York   London*

The text of this book is composed in 10.5/14 ITC Galliard.
Composition by PennSet, Inc.
Manufacturing by Courier Companies Inc.
Book design by Margaret M. Wagner.
Illustration by Michael Chesworth.

Library of Congress Cataloging-in-Publication Data
Stern, Gerald,
Bread without sugar : poems / Gerald Stern.
p.   cm.
I. Title.
PS3569.T3888B7   1992
811'.54—dc20   91-27721
ISBN 0-393-03094-6

W.W. Norton & Company, Inc.
500 Fifth Avenue, New York, N.Y. 10110
W.W. Norton & Company Ltd.
10 Coptic Street, London WC1A 1PU

1 2 3 4 5 6 7 8 9 0

FOR JUDY

Contents

1

Sylvia   *3*
Three Hearts   *5*
The Bull-Roarer   *6*
My Death for Now   *10*
One Day an Arbor Vitae   *12*
Brain of My Heart   *14*
The Founder   *16*
The First Lewd Offering   *18*
Nice Mountain   *19*
Love Is the Opposite   *21*
The Age of Strolling   *23*
Sending Back the Gloom   *26*
One Gift   *29*
First Day of Spring   *31*
R for Rosemary   *37*
How Would It Be?   *39*
Saving My Skin from Burning   *40*
Shouting   *41*
The Eyes Are Always Brown   *43*

2

A Song for Kenneth Burke   *47*
Aspiring to Music   *51*
Grinnell, Iowa   *57*

Ukrainian   *60*
Coleman Valley Road   *61*
What It Is Like   *62*
Two Daws   *64*

3

Her Right Eye Catches the Lavender   *71*
Those Things   *73*
His Song of the Green Willow   *76*
If the Lark Had Thorns   *78*
The Smell of Death   *81*
Red with Pink   *85*
Someone Will Do It for Me   *91*
I Would Call It Derangement   *94*
The Thought of Heaven   *97*

4

Bread Without Sugar   *103*

1

Sylvia

What is Eros doing
standing naked among these gravestones almost
      6,000 miles from Paphos?
What does he want *now*, another handful
      of yellow hair, two blue eyes
and a spine in pain? How is it that he is standing
      without a skullcap on? Does he
think it is he who will bring her in? Does he pine
      for his mama, does he want to
simper, or stamp his foot, or scratch his back
      with his tiny arrow? When was he last
in Pittsburgh, what does he think of these Jews reclining
      off route 51? What is love now
doing with death and what is love now planning
      in such a garden? What is desire
to him—and longing—what, when he lifts her, is in
      his mind?—Where is my plot?—
And where will he take her? Does he think that love
      destroys the world, does he think
that love is death, does he think that love
      should drop his lyre and throw away
his torch, why does he have to be death too
      and carry a vial of mint and a vial
of myrtle? Where does he stash his coins? Where is
      Sylvia's meadow? How is this light the
light par excellence? Why is she buried so close
      to Pete and Jenny Kaplan, was it
a truncated poplar or a truncated cyprus

that stood above her—was it limestone?
Was there a leaf on her tree? Was it too crowded
     in upper K? Eros should trip
over the graves of Libbie and Barrel Barach
     once he starts climbing. Eros should
tell me something; Eros should turn his worms
     around so they face north; he should
decide on one song, then he should sing, or he could
     let the plectrum decide. Eros
should cry when he lifts her, he should have wet cheeks
     this time—how does he get there, does he
land like a fly? What does he think of defilement?
     Eros should have her picture, he should
kiss her curls, he should brush her lips
     with medicine. Who was *his* sister?
How did *his* mama grieve? Is he more heartless
     as love or death? I think Sylvia's own granddaughter
would have touched her cheek and stroked her hair
     as she did her darling Libbie. As I did too.

Three Hearts

A chicken with three hearts, that is a vanished
breed, a day of glory in the corn,
romance against a fence. It was the sunset
just above New Egypt that made me wince,
it was the hay blown up from Lakewood. God
of chance, how much I loved you in those days,
how free I felt and what a joy it was
sitting there with my book, my two knees braced
against the dashboard. How empty it was then,
and how my mind went back. How many hearts
did the chickadee have? How much whistling and singing
was in those fields? How far did I have to go
to disappear in those grasses, to pick those trillium?

The Bull-Roarer

I

I only saw my father's face in butchery
once—it was a horror—there were ten men
surrounding a calf, their faces were red, my father's
eyes were shining; there might have been fewer than ten,
some were farmers, some were my father's friends
down from the city. I was nine, maybe eight;
I remember we slept a few hours and left
at four in the morning, there were two cars, or three,
I think it was West Virginia. I remember
the pasture, the calf was screaming, his two eyes
where white with terror, there was blood and slaver
mixed, he was spread-eagled, there was a rope
still hanging from his neck, they all had knives
or ice picks—is that possible?—they were beery,
drunk, the blood was pouring from the throat
but they were stabbing him, one of them bellowed
as if he were a bull, he was the god
of the hunters, dressed in overalls and boots,
the king of animals; they seemed to know—
some of them seemed to know—the tendons and bones,
they were already cutting and slicing, pulling
the skin off, or maybe that was later, I stood there
staring at them, my father with a knife;
we didn't even have a dog—my mother froze
whenever she saw one—we were living in Beechview,
we had the newest car on the street, it was

an ugly suburb, everything was decent,
there was a little woods, but it was locust,
it would be covered with houses, we didn't even have
a parrot, my father left at eight in the morning
and drove his car downtown, he always wore
a suit and tie, his shoes were polished, he spent
the day with customers, he ate his lunch
at a little booth, I often sat with him,
with him and his friends, I had to show off, I drew
their likenesses, I drew the tables and chairs,
it was the Depression, none of them had brass rings
hanging from their ears, they all wore socks,
and long-sleeved shirts, they ate and drank with passion.

II

My mother is eighty-seven, she remembers
the visit to the farm, there was her brother,
my uncle Simon, and there was his friend, MacBride,
Lou MacBride, he was the connection, he was
a friend of the farmer's, maybe a cousin. I asked her
about the killing—"that is the way those farmers
got their meat, they lived like that, they butchered
whatever they needed." I asked if she could remember
anything strange, was she nervous or frightened?
"There was the tail, they cut the tail off
and chased each other; it was like pinning the tail

to the donkey." Both of us laughed. I didn't have the heart
to mention my father's face, or mention the knife—
and, most of all, my pain. What did I want?
That he should stay forever locked inside
his gold-flecked suits? That he should get up in the dark
and put his shoes on with a silver knife?
That he should unbutton his shirts and stuff the cardboard
into a chute? That he should always tie
his tie with three full loops, his own true version
of the Windsor knot? And what did I want for myself?
Some childish thing, that no one would ever leave me?
That there would always be logic—and loyalty?
—I think that tail goes back to the Paleolithic.
I think our game has gory roots—some cave,
or field, they chased each other—or they were grimmer,
pinning that tail, some power was amassed,
as well as something ludicrous, always that,
the tail was different from the horns, or paws,
it was the seat of shame—and there was envy,
not just contempt, but envy—horns a man has,
and he has furry hands and he has a mane,
but never a tail. I remember dimly
a toy we had, a kind of flattened stone,
curved at the sides, with a long rope at one end
we whirled around to make a thundering noise.
This was a "bull-roarer"; we made thunder
and felt the power in our shoulders and legs.
I saw this toy in southern Italy;

I saw children throwing it over their heads
as if they were in central Australia
or ancient Europe somewhere, in a meadow,
forcing the gods to roar. They call it Uranic,
a heavenly force, sometimes almost a voice,
locked up in that whirling stone, dear father.

My Death for Now

I have settled down to watch the branches
growing vertically from two dead limbs.
It's what I do all day. I raise my left arm
and hunch my shoulder over. My leg is asleep,
which is my death for now, although sometimes
I raise both arms and let the fingers turn on
the vertical branches; then my hands are dead,
not just my leg. It is the middle of January
and there is a sheet of ice and there are berries
and leftover leaves and even a few old weed stalks.
I wave my fingers—there is a little wind—
I arch my neck—there is a twisted trunk
against a wire fence. It is a window
I sit in. I am marking a day for wisdom.
I give that to myself. I give myself
a day for mercy. I turn my hand around;
it is an amaryllis. The wrist is bent,
the fingers are spread. I give myself a basket;
I brought it from Pennsylvania; I put the flower
inside the basket. The wire is gorgeous. The handle
was rubbed by German farmers. It was filled
by yellow peaches. There is a certain dryness
that makes them small and juicy. Too much rain
will make them mealy, or stringy. I touch my lips
to the little leaves; it is the flower of fruits,
delicate, aromatic, yet they are heavy,
they weigh the basket down. I stretch my palms;
I look at them in awe. I straighten my fingers.

I bend for water. I drink the snow. I lie
on my stomach drinking snow. Two of the peaches
are bruised. I turn them around. I try to keep them
free of each other. I do it by concentration.
I blink one eye; and frown. That is the dream,
just sitting and thinking—frowning; that is the joke,
the juices running down. I bend like a bee,
I lean to the left, one hand is at my neck,
the other is on my cheek. I wipe my chin.
I may as well count the leaves—buried in the snow;
I might as well listen to the diesels or bring the
squirrels back and watch them dig. That was September,
the end of summer, my window was open, a dwarf
was singing in my bedroom, there were books
spread all over the porch, with pencils inside,
there were mosquitoes still, my birch was turning,
the noise was insane, birds were screaming, walnuts
were dropping on the roof. I might as well die
from the past; I might as well die from longing.

One Day an Arbor Vitae

I always went for natural shapes, I slid
on the mud to get away from my street, I ripped
my leather jacket on the hill hanging on
to a broken branch; I swung there, one foot turned,
one foot almost lost. It took me an hour
to find a certain willow; I say an hour
but it was more like twenty minutes. I went
to the roundhouse and back in fifteen or twenty minutes,
I went to the station itself in half an hour.
Six in the morning was my time, I picked up
three kinds of grass, I wrapped them in my notebook.
Once there was a truck, it was called
a stakesider, I think the bed lifted up;
the wheels were scattered, the cab was gone, a kind of
Eastern tumbleweed hung from the axle.
Once there was an opossum broken in two,
the head was wet from the rain, the tongue was rolling,
there was a pool of water in the thorax.

I always went to the bridge and back, there was a
white angora on the tracks, her bell
was jingling; I tried to keep her away from the carcass,
I tried to help the crows. There was a tire
buried in the mud, someone had thrown it
down, the leaves were planted inside it; I knelt there
hating the cat. I read the Sunday paper
standing on the rubbish. I broke a stick
before I climbed the hill, it helped me think,

one day it was a sword, one day a crutch,
one day it was a broom. I held it up
with two of my fingers, I smashed some branches, I cut
some ugly roots, it helped me sleep at night,
having it there beside my bed, leaving it
behind the door, either inside or outside.
One day it was an insect, one day a flutist
leaning with one arm out and one leg splattered;
one day an arbor vitae, one day a maple.

Brain of My Heart

Thank God for the walnut in 1986.
Thank God for the hard green shell and the greasy center.
All you, you thirty white worms and forty green grubs,
I know what you are, burrowing like pigs,
running like moles inside your bulging rooms.

I pick up a rubber ball, it may be a walnut
gone black on the sidewalk, it may have a hundred worms
drinking the juices and drying up the husks.
I do a Pittsburgh twist, a double-handed
reverse action, I learned it in three short hours.
I put my foot on the mound, the rubber juices
fall like blood on the street; I'm doing the fiend's work;
I kick the tennis balls. I drive my car
over the hard green stones, it is the bounce
I learned in Philadelphia, pebbles piled up
in every alley, a terrible screaming and wailing.

Deep in the recesses two yellow brains
are facing each other. They are like human brains,
the hills and valleys make an expanded surface,
the neurons are popping, the chemicals are charging,
the eyes are already staring, the mouth is running.

Deep in the recesses there is a Twelfth Crusade.
A murderous knight is already on his knees.
His right eye is gone, his left arm is lopped at the wrist,
the skin is sewn together. He is back

in Europe. He has given up. His murders
will take five years to repay, his shoulder is raw
from the leather. There are two heads at his belt,
he has combed their hairs. Their little tongues
are whispering, one has the grating voice
of Billie Holiday, one has the voice
of Jimmy Durante, one is tormented, one
is full of sappy wisdom. It is freezing,
winter has come in one day, the few brown leaves
will turn to pieces of ice. I start to huddle
inside my blanket. I start to store my blood,
my brain is moving south, my mind is wandering.

The Founder

There was a kind of drooping bronze head
I stole in the Catskills and put in my living room
in Philadelphia. I put a sledge hammer
beside it so my friends and I could smash him
and change his shape from thoughtful oppressor
to tortured victim. This was just to show
the close connection between the two, the liquid
life of Capitalism; we got to kick him,
we got to gouge his eyes out, we were elated
breaking his nose and flattening his ear; it was
a kind of funeral rite, sometimes the hammer
hummed in our hands, there was a jolt, his pain
was in our wrists; sometimes we were exhausted
from so much pounding; after a while his face
was old and twisted, it was a little shameful.
I finally sold him—by the pound, I think;
he was too ugly for us, too demented;
we were starting to turn to pity—we pitied
that bronze bastard, he who must have presided
over the burning of mountains, he who managed
the killing of souls, the death of every dream.

I reached inside once to get the brain
but it was only rough casting in there,
nothing to suck on, even though the cavity
was widened at the base of the skull. He was
a brainless founder, his eyes stared at the wall,
or if we turned him around his eyes stared

with a kind of wonder at the dining-room table
catching the pools of beer. I remember
it wasn't all raw Socialism and hatred
of the rich; there was a little terror in it.
I think sometimes I got out of bed early
and put a towel or a T-shirt over his face
to cover his eyes and his ugly deformities.
He was for a while a mutilated ancestor,
someone we had buried twice, a monster,
something that could ruin us. It took an effort
to put him on the back of a station wagon
and free ourselves from fright. I had to struggle.
Although I'm sorry I sold him, he deserved
to be buried somewhere. I should have driven
to one of the dumps and thrown him into a valley
between a sofa and a refrigerator,
or just gone into the woods and made a grave
between two birches and shoved him in. I'm glad
there wasn't a river; I would have dropped him
down in the muck with the black Budweiser,
and one cold spring the current would have carried him
through a park or into a muddy backyard
on top of the poison and the wild strawberries,
or carried him into the open, his crushed head
going faster and faster, turning around in the garbage,
his face forever swollen, his eyes squinting,
the sorrow coming from his metal lips,
the sun shining down, the melodies never ending.

The First Lewd Offering

I am one of the squirrels—I have a dogwood
in my breast pocket, I am *smitten*, I squeeze
the four red corners back together, I make
a purse to hold the seeds again. I tried
to *pluck* the flower, to snap it off, but there was
rage in the branches, there was glue, I had to
pull the wood loose, there is such brute strength
in a blossom. I had no idea the mouth
was in those leaves or there was a yellow brain
half buried under ground. I walk with greed
up every mountain, there is always a mark
of courtesy between us, I could turn it
to love if I wanted, the ground is so soft, the branches
are all so careful. There were thorns getting here,
there was water—at first—up to my ankles,
there was a wire fence. I lean my head
against a hemlock. There is no loyalty.
The honeysuckle will come, then the catalpa.
I will drink the nectar, I will study
the magic prints, one out of four is crimson—
it is the blood, I guess. If there was a tree
that kept me sane I know it was that one; if there
was a life it was that life. I first got the blossoms
in a brown envelope, the *blossoms* were brown—
and dry—I put them on my dashboard; that was
the first lewd offering; I was forgiven.

Nice Mountain

Great little berries in the dogwood,
great little *buds*, like purple lights
scattered through the branches, perfect wood
for burning, three great candelabra
with dozens of candles, great open space
for sun and wind, great view, the mountain
making a shadow, the river racing
behind the weeds, great willow, great shoots,
great burning heart of the fields, nice leaves
from last year's crop, nice veins and threads,
nice twigs, mostly red, some green and silky,
nice sky, nice clouds, nice bluish void.

I light my candles, I travel quickly
from twig to twig, I touch the buttons
before I light them—it is my birthday,
two hundred years—I count the buds,
they come in clusters of four and seven,
some are above me, I gather a bunch
and hold it against my neck; that is
the burning bush to my left, I pick
some flaming berries, I hang them over
my tree, nice God, nice God, the silence
is broken by the flames, the voice
is a kind of tenor—there is a note
of hysteria—I came there first,
I lit the tree myself, I made
a roaring sound, for two or three minutes

I had a hidden voice—I try
to blow the candles out, nice breath,
nice wagon wheel, great maple, great chimes,
great woodpile, great ladder, great mound of tires,
nice crimson berries, nice desert, nice mountain.

Love Is the Opposite

I carry the white head with me
and stare at it eye to eye. I'd say it's a
bobcat, not an opossum, I'd say it
trembled for half an hour once in a sweet gum
before it jumped; I'd say an opossum
had softer teeth, a flatter jaw, I'd say
that anger drifted through the species, that we were
lucky we learned it from the cats. For my part
I sit on a silken couch, there is a bolt
of extra cloth in the cellar once the stain
covers these cushions. If I had a tree
it would be a cottonwood, one long trunk,
to claw my way up, to hump and then pull, a narrow
limb, covered with leaves, for my two eyes
to hide behind, my eyes and my shoulders. Love
is the opposite, some kind of love, maybe tenderness,
maybe regret. I dig my claws in, the pads
would be enough but I have nails; I scream—
that is my way—I watch the curtains blow.
It takes a year for the flesh to go, for rage
to be reduced to fluff; some time next summer
I will be bleached—ah Yorick, I know you well,
you carried me in your pocket, ah opossum,
I carried *you*; your skull is the size of an apple,
my pockets are full, they are like cheeks; oh bobcat,
bobcat, you were betrayed, you are unloved,
you rage at yourself, you are an accomplice; oh bobcat,
you are in grief—and frightened—it is your death

you lick, you are humiliated, the stars
discarded you, the clouds withdrew. For a year
you shook, the leaves of the cottonwood curled up
as if the ground had lost its water. I know it
so well, for a year I shivered, and sighed, oh rabbit.

The Age of Strolling

I loved a certain period; I wore
an overcoat that came down to my ankles.
I carried a stick—a cane—I had that stiffness.
Now, to this day, whenever I take a picture,
I pose as if I were living then. I take
the world in with a glance, although you'd think
my eyes were riveted on a pin of light
or to a streak of dirt. There was a way
we ate then, there was a way we walked, we trundled,
we rolled, the hips in a line with the shoulders; it was
an age of strolling—who knows that word?—you lift
one leg at a time, your toes are pointed out,
your shoes have crease after crease. There were our cities,
there were our railroad stations, there were our newspapers,
Switzerland was our country. We used to sit there
behind our panes of glass; those were our mountains
we stared at, those were our crude and dirty cities.
Always there was one drama. I am spending
my life on that. I have the magazines,
I have the photographs. I think it was fear.
I used to call it happiness—nervousness—
that's what it was. My book was always Job.
Where can wisdom be found? Could we go out
and scrub some building down, a Gothic high school
with garbage on the staircase, one old light bulb
hanging from a wire? There in the branches
is Absalom the beautiful. A mule
was his undoing, he rode it into the woods

and he was taken up between heaven and earth.
It was a mule of great stupidity;
it was a prince of loveliness. They stuck
spears in his body; they were tipped with metal
to make him hemmorhage more; he was murdered
and buried in the woods. How could his head
be lifted up like that? Was it his hair
that ruined him? How could he hang without a word?
David was sitting in the gate; he saw
a messenger crawling across the field, he thought
it's like a beetle; he thought, it's like an ant;
there should be something white, there should be black,
there should be a bird. He climbed into the room
above the gate. He thought of Absalom's mother.
His body began to shake—the king of music—
he thought of the Philistine giants. What is a giant?
He thought of Saul. How just he had been. He thought
of Bathsheba—and poor Uriah. What was his God
doing to him? Where would the messenger stand?
Should he not kneel? Should he not prostrate himself?
—I think myself there was a trap; Absalom
was snapped up into the sky. I saw a zebra
hanging like that—a photograph. Life
in 1887 was different. I heard
the *Symphony Pathétique* last night. Forgive me
for saying this, I loved the gloom itself.
What joy there was to settle into that sadness,
to sit in the first row of the balcony

and hold my hand on my breast, to stand on the steps
and talk for a minute about Tchaikovsky's death,
to solve the secret suicide, to smile
over the scandal and the vicious code,
to say goodbye—in the street—to hold my glove
so the fingers fell against the palm, to walk
across the river, to stop in the middle, to lean
facing east where all the bridges were—that pleasure.
It started when I was twenty. As I recall
I walked across the Sixth Street bridge, there were
the row houses first and then the mansions; I walked
on the wooden porches and looked into the windows.
I studied the gas lamps and the wallpaper.
I loved it when there was no *conversion*. I was
already sacrificing. I was a slave
or I was a ghost. This has been
a long distracted life. I have carried
my secrets with me. That is my explanation.
When I stood there cupping my right hand
and when I looked at the barges struggling up
my river I was already changed. I spent
a lifetime doing this, grieving and arguing.

Sending Back the Gloom

for Kerry Keys

One time I rose from my bed, I had to walk
to the bridge and back, I had to listen to water
move under me. There was a tree to look at,
it was a dead tree, really a giant stump,
with a bird hole in the back and a dangling wing.
—It is three miles to the bridge and back, a little
under maybe, but "three" is convenient; I walk
as if I were running, I slow down only once
to wait for the cows or study the shredded sky.
I dream of my drink—boiled sumac—the juices
are drained through cheese cloth, the long hairs and the pulp
are left behind; I drink it as I walk.
It is the hawthorn I wanted—I have a thorn
in one of my pockets, it is a toothpick—the hawthorn
leans to one side—I have seen it—the branches
are close together, sometimes touching, dense
is what the Field Guide calls it, almost a shrub,
perfect for nesting, sometimes hundreds of birds
fly out of a single tree, sometimes they huddle
and shriek all day in the midst of their fruit and flowers.
—I lean on my elbows when I reach the bridge;
I dangle my wrists, I spread my fingers, I stare at
the water, the river curves through an open field,
there are no banks, there are no obstacles.
I love that kind of river, the water and the land
are level with each other; I don't know
if a river like that can have a name, or if
it's a river at all; if there's a flood the water

will spread over half an acre, maybe the curving
is what I like, the endless curving; the walk
back is different, the sky is purple and the sun
is lighting the fields, the sumac is on my left,
the hawthorn is on my right; I reach for a straw,
I reach for a stick of grass, I pass the Texas
pipeline, I stop in a valley, the sky is over me,
the trees are close, every ten yards the view
is different; I count up to seven colors, the day
is over at 3 o'clock, the last half mile
I walk through the woods, the dead tree is on a hillside
on top of me—it is a hummock—a rusted
wire fence runs through one side, the bark,
what there is of it, is dry and gray, the wood
is rotten, you can pull it off in pieces,
or you can pull the bark off separately.
Dirt is piled up inside, it keeps the tree
together, dirt and leaves and grass—it must be
twenty feet tall from top to bottom; from the front
it is a piece of sculpture, Garibaldi
with one arm in the air, Demosthenes
cursing the Blue Mountains; from the rear
it is a one-eyed monster, the bird hole
is thick and protruding, there the graceful and pleading
arm is almost invisible; I carry
a thorn in one hand, a scarred branch in the other,
the flowers are gone, this isn't one of the limbs
that bloom all winter, white and brown memories

of dreams gone by; half of my life is pleasure
and half of it is dread, I turn my corner
shouting to myself, the smoke is pouring
from eleven chimneys, we are sending back
the gloom, I hold my branch up, it is unlucky
to sing in this tree, or underneath it, I hang
my hat from the thorn, I look like a florist crossing
the highway, I am branched and perfumed.

One Gift

If I have one gift it is rising in the dark
and falling to my death down a vertical stairway.

It is walking with my feet spread out in both directions
and pressing the white plaster with my red fingers.

One time I was paralyzed, my leg disappeared,
and there was mist between my right knee and the floor.

One time I rose to the ceiling. I closed like a knife
after banging my head against the gritty stucco.

Sometimes there is fleece, the sheets are in shreds
and a white face is floating over the window;

sometimes there is blood, my hand is sticky,
the back of my head is wet, my mouth is salty.

Blood is my terror, blood just under the skin,
blood in the toilet, blood on the pillow. I hear

of every disgrace. I shake from fear. I hate
the heart being where it is, a piece of leather

covered with jelly, pressed against the backbone;
I hate the rotten lungs; I feel like a chicken

lying open, there is a speck of liver
above the gall—what pain if I were alive!—

what sadness there is for the spirit! There is the rope
that carries thought, there is love behind

the bladder. Down I go on one knee.
Sometimes I snore; I do that while I am lying,

it is my other gift. I crawl outside
to get at the moon. There is a balcony

over my head. I should be up there moaning.
Sometimes I end up wandering, sometimes sleeping.

First Day of Spring

for Bruce and Fox McGrew

I have been such a follower,
first Porphyry, then Alexander,
I have gone so long without shaving,
that now I have nothing
except this mustache and this forked stick.
Behold one T-shirt
I have traveled with from one wrinkled continent to the other;
behold one leg
that lifted me up over 40,000 thresholds.
My heart—such as it was—
always surprised me,
and my curved back,
it never gave out on the stairway,
it never paused once in spite of
the lifeless ankle
and the unlubricated lung.

There was a red carpet once
in the north of France
that wandered like a river
from the staircase to the first turn
and lapped against the plastered walls.
I stood outside a door
listening to two cries,
one gutteral and despairing,
one frantic and birdlike.
I shifted my trunk to my left shoulder
and began another climb,

three steps to the landing,
sixteen or eighteen steps to the next river.
As far as I can remember,
even with the closing of the door
and the admiration of my own face
in the unsilvered mirror,
stuck as it was wrongly
between two loose pillars
on a mahogany wardrobe,
I listened to their cries
half with shame, half with desire,
and half with terror and half with unabashed regret.

That was the beginning of grief,
the start of a second life,
although it wasn't that
the love cries themselves did this,
it wasn't the moaning—
or the creaking floor
or the exploding pipes—
it was, for the first time in *my* life,
I was abandoned.
I had to grab some rail
or vestigial fixture
sticking out of the wall
and do a shaky dance
under the heavy trunk.
I was suspended.

I guess I lay on the bed
staring at the ceiling
and the painted wire going into the light bulb,
or I guess I lay there remembering—
although I know I cut short the first years
and I know I concentrated on the early tribes,
crying out with rage and disappointment
in their slide from shelf to shelf;
though what I should have done,
and what I was able to do later,
was smile at what they *did* do
in the 200,000 years,
the first half aeon.
It took me one decade
till I could lie peacefully,
and two or more—
I think it was three or more—
to forgive myself,
or just to ignore myself,
for singing at the wrong time,
for interrupting the way I do,
for moaning, for talking out loud,
for being a dwarf.

In the great and lasting argument
that overwhelmed the Mediterranean
for more than a thousand years
I took the losing side.

I would do that in Spain
in the time of the two Sulimans
and I would do that in America
in the time of the two Stevensons.
I wanted to mourn for kings,
I wanted a bonnie prince,
and I wanted to feel the stinging
salt on my face too—
the silent ship, the sym-
pathetic sailors, the letters
wrapped in leather, a bottle
waiting to be opened,
a ribbon around the neck.
I solved problem after problem
in 1985
in the *campo dei fiore*
not only at the fish stand
but in the freezing movie house
where we sat in leather coats
and rocked in our chairs
watching the Blues Brothers
in English and Italian.
This is where Bruno died,
this is where my foot dragged
on the way to the river,
this is where Brutus—may
the Lord keep him insane—
swam before eating.

My favorite church
both then and now
was Il Gesù
where the Jews were herded together on Holy Thursday
to listen to a sermon
on the joys of conversion,
only a few blocks away
from the Vesuvio Palace, my
own crowded bakery.

It was astounding
to walk up that red carpet
in the fifth decade,
and it was astounding
to rock by the river
in the middle of the eighth.
Something was in my mind
both then and then
and something later brought it back again.
Sometimes you wait for forty years, it was
a little less for me
when I first thought of Alexander and Porphyry.
I have forgotten now, but I remember
it was a sweet elation, I was happy
and I was half-suspended.
                        I am sitting
in Arizona, the moon is full, so check
the twenty-first of March 1989.

I was reading Horace tonight, who never
wrote by porchlight, maybe a dish of oil
outside Brindisi. Ah, the stricken soul,
he sat till midnight waiting for a girl
who never came. I love his *sense*, he knew
where the ludicrous lay, he hated
quackery. I wonder
if maybe in the palace he had seen
a bromeliad once and touched the drooping flower—
the rubbery claws; I wonder if he talked
to a passing fox about the frogs that lived
in those leaves, if he had exchanged some wisdom, how
it only eats air, how it clings to palm trees; I wonder
if March twenty-first was when the plum tree bloomed
in Tivoli, if he had also seen
hundreds of butterflies in those branches, if he
lay down and wept—in spite of his careful mind—
if that is the third suspension, the third abandonment.

R for Rosemary

I heard a fluttering—just inside the door
of my *casita*; it was inside a bush,
a kind of pine, a kind of blue rosemary,
and since I saw two doves wandering under
my window yesterday and over my stones
I thought there had to be a mourning dove—
or two of them—puffed up and asleep,
living inside that bush, one of them frightened
by my loud steps. But I will know them later
by their sweet smell, whether they stretch their necks
or stick their chests out, getting ready to soar,
for they have made the mistake of living in rosemary
and they are spies for now and carry the stench
of betrayal on them. I could have reached inside
and heard them scream and watch the bushes shudder
with terror, but I let them go. More
and more I do that. Why did I wait so long
to let them have their darkness? I rub the leaves
under my chin and over my wrists. I know
the smell will last. I crawl up under my window
and try my keys. I'll have to pull the blinds
and close the curtains, those doves are so rotten; they are
such eavesdroppers. We listen to each other
through the glass, we preen in our mirrors; their cooing
is absurd, it is the noisy sound
of codex international; I know
the tapping, I know the turning of the head;
and it is odd to watch them stretch a wire

between their beaks and under my windowsill,
then walk off unaffected. I put powder
over my shoes. I know that trick. I called it
blue rosemary because of the flowers, I should have
called it lavender; it was my color
when I was a boy; there were *two* doves; we wandered
from bush to bush, it was a disease of the spine
that took the other one; she was a dove. If I
spend year after year explaining it is because
I was left without her. I have a sprig
of the dried-up plant, the leaves and the flowers have mixed,
the color is greenish-blue, almost an olive;
it has some weight, the woody part is heavy,
it is itself a kind of flattened tree;
it is a bookmark; it is a perfumed wing.

How Would It Be?

How would it be at my age to burn some land
between a Chinese willow and a white mulberry?

What would I do with the smoke
that blows first toward the television wires

and then reverses itself to curl some flowers
still hanging from the dwarf apple?

Couldn't my love be in that fire, wouldn't she
just adore those ashes, wouldn't she just love to stir

a stick in that dust, and wouldn't she love to dream
of another birth and another conversion?

Couldn't she get on her knees? Couldn't she also
smear her face with dirt? Couldn't she explode?

Saving My Skin from Burning

There was a hole in the ground once; there was a manhole
I used to get inside. I lowered a rope
and kicked my way down. The walls were two feet thick
and there was at most a foot of leaves where somehow
the wind had crept in, but there was no water. I felt for
the pipe, there was a little ledge—with matches.
I tried to get out. The truth was I fell. My mind
was on vipers, I called my enemies vipers, it was
an old honorific word but now I shook,
they were not just snakes—they were adders—their bodies
were flat, their fangs were huge, my enemies
strike like they do—their heads are triangles,
their eyes are in their skulls. I screamed for rope,
I needed rags, I had to save my skin
from burning—my chest and upper arms.
                                    The hole
is our greatest fear; I grab the air behind me
and stiffen my legs. The greatest joy is rising,
the greatest joy is resting your arms on the ground
and getting ready to swing your body up—
and seeing the clouds again and feeling the wind
on your white legs, and rubbing your eyes. I ran
to touch a tree, I stroked the bark, there was
one stone, it was half-pitted, the sun had turned it
into a pillow; I lay on my back recovering.

Shouting

Now I am reading a psalm,
the lack of mercy here and there,
doves freezing in the doorway.

I sink into something,
water covers me up to my neck,
my throat is burning.

It is a joy like this,
more fat than blind, more blind
than deaf, though that is coming. Either I fly

or I walk, but either way there is no sweetness.
Give me back, it says,
the brilliance of early October. I turn blue

when I think of it. The sun made a shadow on the wall,
the moon had a nimbus. I think of it and I moan.
My breath falters. I keep going back and back.

First there was fear, though I never called it
that, then there was silence. First there was sadness,
then there was anger. There is snow on my roof;

it makes me think of justice. I go back
over and over again. The white footprints
have nothing exactly to do with it. They lie

between the trees, the powder fills them up.
I make one turn—it doesn't matter—I could have
made another. There is a rock, it is

a teacher, it is a shield. I start to sing
a song with my hands; there is a pool of hot water;
I sit there with the rest; this is going back

with a vengeance; life was boiling; what we lacked
was a nucleus; we ate sulphur; there was light
twelve miles away; there was a great disorder.

What good is pity? I shake the needles; snow
slides down my neck. What I sing is buried.
I walk on the left side three or four miles a day,
shouting.

The Eyes Are Always Brown

I spend an hour watching the yellow parrots
swooping in and out of the jacaranda;
I touch each building with an oar; I count
the cars going by—I have a system—I watch
through a window, I see them go into the chairs
and over the vase of flowers; the brass coupling
helps me line them up and steer them through.
There is a bird of paradise here, his cheeks
are like a duck's, although the web is too long;
his crest is like a cockatoo's; a flower
grows out of his skull; his neck is buried. And there is
a fish nearby, her nose is purple, spots
of gold run up and down her body, her tail
is red, her teeth are absurdly small, her fins
are almost demented.
                  I am starting a trip
on the east side of Vandam; I travel south,
although the traffic flows north. I have no qualms—
in fact there is a certain delight. The sun,
what there is of it, is shining on the library
of the blind; the subway shakes my bench, I sit
holding the gunnels; one of my hands is dragging
through the orchids. I am making the sound
of the magpie; there are silken feces floating
in front of me, there is a wave, I smash
a pale scorpion with my palm, I touch
two windowsills. It is the same woman
staring at me, the flowers are always yellow,

the eyes are always brown—or was it chocolate?—
that made me bend over and gasp. I tip my helmet,
it is a *casque*, I offer her sink water,
I offer her bread and cheese, my table is set,
here is a napkin for her. I pass by
and lift my hand a little; I have a foolish
smile. I will have to make a decision
in one or two minutes, either I'll stop on an island
or drift down to the wall. I'll never see her
again, or the jacaranda; we call it death,
we call it worse than death; there was a hook
inside the heart against both walls; the brain
is the best organ for love; more than drifting
I love this jouncing. I give a piece of cheese
to the drowned fish; I'll never see the accountant
with the white cuffs, I'll never see the bus driver.
My back is red from bending over; the sun
is pouring down; I sprinkle a little water
over my head, over the fish's head.
I'll never crash into Kleinsleep. Should I have brought
a harp? What do they have here? What if they planted
harps, what if they knelt in the sand and prayed
to the strings? What is the moon doing now,
drifting through the water towers? Why
did I stop to listen to that music, poor love?

2

of her baby—how could those limbs be perfect
like that? How could those blossoms come
again and again? The whole tree is covered
with flowers. Poor Burke! When he finally gets here
there will be just a white rug, but that
is something too. I see him bend down—
the last time I saw him his legs were crooked—
and pick up a blossom. He holds it to his eye,
he blows on the edges. I heard he lived
in a cottage in west New Jersey, it is
ramshackle, no electricity,
a bottle of vodka on the sink,
the papers piled up, a stand of trees
outside the window, little hills
to soothe his spirit, a hand-dug pond—
with pickerel—a tiny sand beach,
with rushes, for Moses, so Moses can lie there
planning the future. My apples are yellow,
and hard and sweet; I eat them all day;
some are rotten, all are rotten
a little; I love a wrinkled skin,
I love the seeds. I pick some flowers—
it's early still—I'll put them in a vase—
with lilacs—I'll arrange them. This is
my month: tulips, lilacs, cherries—
and violets—under the apple—green
and purple and white; this is the month—
under our lake and near our river—

for plans, for visions; not September,
not December.
                    Burke had a plan
to call things by their other name;
it was an exotic plan. He lived
near hills and water; that was in the blood,
that was in the mind; he lived
by moonlight—there is another race
among us; he was almost Li-Po
for a minute; he pursued that face
for years, he stalked a soul, he cried
in Greek, he spoke to a shadow, he dropped
a stone in the pond, a part of him shivered,
it almost exploded; he spoke to the moon
with caution. Who is to say the moon
loved one of them less? How could you not
turn into a shadow? What would that fish
now eat? What if it nibbled on his hair?
What if it swam through his eye? Sustenance
is in the brain. How could Burke not
derive his knowledge from the talk
in drugstores—was the fish not brainfood?
Didn't the pickerel swim in the mind?
Was there not a reversal? Didn't
the pickerel eat that meal? Was gray food
not what he ate? Did he not gobble
blood and nerves? Did he not dip

his nose into the skull, was he
not a fish of fury?
                    Burke bends down
to pick up a porous stick, he sensed
the lightness, it shone in the moonlight, the holes
were there for the light to come through though water
took over sometimes and mud caked up
his exits—for him they were exits. He floats
his stick, it is another face;
a third; a fourth if you count the moon;
he should have put some feathers on
the forehead and scarred the cheeks. He runs
to the other side, the grasses scratch
his ankles, his slippers are soaked, he picks up
his stick; the water is black, the roots run
into his fingers. For just a minute
he thought of Thales—he could be Thales
explaining the world. Was he not Thales?
Did he not have one explanation—
and then another? If he had a glass
he'd lift it to the moon. Ah, vodka,
with ice. Vermouth. What if love
could be reduced? What are the words
in German and Hebrew? How did the Greeks
help lead him astray? How long did his Lucy
wait? What is the word for sorrow?
What is the word for live fish, for shadow?

Aspiring to Music

My favorite piece of dreck
on the grasses of Houston Street
is a bottle of Bohemia,
green and shiny on the outside,
brown and watery on the inside.

Or the grille of a Mercedes
sitting on the curb,
slightly bent on the left,
slightly haughty, its steel nose
finally up in the air.

I count two hundred pieces
between Thompson and Sullivan,
some of them monstrous and baffling,
some of them dropped from the moon,
all of it oily and dirty.

Today, kind Lord, the mayor
was voted out. In a week
his brilliant ventures in the world
of Thought will be forgotten
and we will have our lives back.

Down there in Tompkins Square
a little cheer will go up
in front of the makeshift hospital

and in the open tents
lining the circular walks.

If I stay too long I'll either
faint from the fumes or I'll die
from the noise—this island is narrow;
I feel the wind from the trucks,
I feel the weight of the tires.

I work up a dance—I always
do that—paper napkins
and broken glass. Dance
and poetry are the close ones,
and all that shameful talk

about poetry and music
is just a high-pitched raving
from one philosopher
to another, one vile German,
one berserk mayor.

Music and poetry
are enemies; the sounds
I make come from my twenty-
stringed tongue. The vile ones hate
not only words but the crude

sources; they hate the tongue,
they hate the blood on those strings,
they hate the sorrow; dancing
they never did, poetry
they never wrote, but they

played piano, and violin.
Poor Coleridge—even Coleridge
submitted. What did *he* play,
the flute? Did Wordsworth play
a little harp? Why is music

the measure? I have met
a ravishing dancer—how
do you say that with notes? It takes
twenty-seven minutes to walk
from Thompson and Houston to Saint

Mark's Place and Avenue A,
the left side of Tompkins, the center
of Bombay, the absolute horror
of the known world. One time I was stuck there
with the other pieces of paper.

I didn't know how to get out,
I couldn't find the gate,
I finally walked through the playground

and ended up going west
instead of east. You have to

be locked in to under-
stand—they didn't even hate me,
they didn't even hate the mayor,
they didn't even hate the mosquitoes,
they were aspiring to music;

not only art—all things
aspire to music. Just ask
a piece of paper. They sat there
in a quiet mode; it was
the hour of reason, some

were smoking tea, some
were sleeping. For how many years
have I been walking like this?
For how many years have I
been dancing and singing? I cross

in front of two trucks; I feel
the heat; I could have sat
in the grass, I could have put up
a tent. How long would they let me
stay? What is the ordinance

forbidding housekeeping? Would I
have gotten support? What prophet
would be my model? What psalm
would I sing? There were four grasses
on that plot—I take

some heart in that. Here is
the toothpick I plucked; it's almost
like wheat. I could have grown
tomatoes—that is for me
the mark of a habitation;

I would have searched for worms
for an hour each morning; I would have
planted my marigolds
in a perfect circle. I have
almost enough money now

to stop my wandering.
I certainly have enough
to live on a grass plot
in the middle of Houston Street
and more than enough to print

some words for the sorrowful
or give away three dollars
a day—that makes a thousand

a year—will you give a thousand
a year to the sorrowful?

I dedicate this poem
to the woman in blue who preached
neighborhood mercy last Sunday
on Sixth near Twenty-first.
I also dedicate it

to the carp on Bleecker Street
who lived in the bleached grasses
underneath the lilies
and fed on the floating pods,
the bloated sunflecked carp.

Grinnell, Iowa

Guy Daniels would have loved May
if he could see those teachers coming toward him
with baked chicken and white wine in their arms.
He would have bent down a little
and closed his eyes the way he did
to smell a lilac or a wet spirea.
When I drive through those empty streets or past
the giant feed stores and storage sheds
I think of how he lived in New York, the shame
of all those steps, the uncontrolled steam, the terrible
darkness of his rooms. I have heard him
rage against five administrations. I have
listened to his jokes—in French and Russian—
and I have heard him shout at three wives and anger
his few friends with his endless self-pity
but I have never heard him talk about this state
with anything but affection. When I drive
four times over the Iowa River, because
it twists underneath our highways, I half-see
Guy Daniels in 1941 just starting
a life in the East, some precious books, a few
shirts and ties, a smile on his face, a young
man's gloom and purity surrounding him
like a white cloud, the cloud of steam that goes by
his unwashed window. I half-see him changing
trains in Chicago, his suitcase is on his shoulder,
his coat is open. The war is what ruined him, Nixon
ruined him, living three years in Washington, living

by his wits in New York City, the best translator
of Russian in America; leaving Iowa,
forgetting the River Road outside Ottumwa,
forgetting the streaks of lightning over the Capitol.

Walking toward those teachers my eyes water
as if I were Guy Daniels. I half-bow
to show respect. I keep thinking it is
the second decade of the twentieth century,
or maybe as late as 1940. I bend
to pick a few spring beauties, they are scattered
like what? like snow? snow in May? They last
one hour I think; I give them to the tall
wife in the linen dress; she would have adored
me once; I can hear a cardinal; there is
nest after nest in the woods; I think of the steamliner
racing toward Cedar Falls, but I am
once removed—I am not Daniels—I think of
the stone hills in the north, the black trucks
pointed into the curb, the bitter farm
holidays, the empty corn palace.

I pick a poppy—made of paper—it is
the color of the one I buy each year
May thirtieth, or the Monday before.
I pull a caterpillar from my shirt;
I give him another home, a green leaf
surpassing all green leaves; I watch him with a straw,

a kind of supple vein I took from a leaf
the next one over to his. I keep away ants
and birds. He is half bursting with desire,
he almost is ready for his molt, he almost
is ready for his week of rage and sorrow.

Ukrainian

for Robin Beeman

Before I go outside I daub my face
with vinegar. That is Ukrainian. I put
one drop behind my knee and one on my earlobe.
I choose a bush. If there is a flower I scatter
a grain of sugar on the twig to help
the flying worms; I pick a weed; I prop
a rain-drenched tulip. There is a part of me
that lives forever. Spring after spring I sit
at my redwood table; at this point the grain is white
with age, the boards are splintered, the hole that held
a grand umbrella is bent, or twisted, nothing
could fit there. Yet I'm enchanted. I sit on the bench—
one of two—half-curved—the table itself
is round, it measures more than a yard, the end boards
are split and shattered. I have one favorite tree
and one favorite bird. I lift my cocoa. Water
is all around me. I make a pact; if the tree
lasts one more year, if it blooms next spring, if the flowers
that cover the twigs and fill the sky come back again
I'll stay here another winter, I'll plant a garden,
I'll trim my branches, I'll rake my leaves. The cardinal
who lives beside the redbud, he whose crimson
is richer than that pink, he who almost
shames the tulips, he whose carnal cry
is always loud and florid, he is my witness.

Coleman Valley Road

This is where I had my sheep vision,
in the brown grass, under the stars.
I sat there shivering, fumbling with my paper,
losing tobacco. I was a spark at the most,
hanging on to my glasses, trying to hide
from the wind. This is how I bent

my head between my knees, the channels and veins
pumping wildly, one leg freezing, one leg
on fire. That is the saxophone
and those are the cymbals; when it gets up here
the roar of the waves is only a humming, a movement
back and forth, some sloshing we get used to.

That is my cello music and those are my headlights
making tunnels in the grass; those are
the clouds going down and those are the cliffs going out.
I am reaching up. I think I have
a carp's face, I have a round nose
and a large red eye and a ragged white mustache.

The strings are stretched across the sky; one note
is almost endless—pitiless I'd say—
except for the slight sagging; one note is
like a voice, it almost has words, it sings
and sighs, it cracks with desire, it sobs with fatigue.
It is the loudest sound of all. A shrieking.

What It Is Like

I will have to tell you what it is like
since I was the one lying on my back
with my arms in the air and a blanket up to my
chin, since I was the one on a mattress
and the one trying to make up my mind
whether it was an early heaven just being there
or whether it was another bitter vertigo.

There were great parties where I went out
on a back porch and stared through the sycamores,
and there were parties, mostly lawless gatherings,
where we stood on the beach apart from each other
studying the sky. For me it's always
the earth; I'm one of the addicts; I can hardly
stand the dreaminess; I get burnt, I blister

at night as others do in the day. Last summer
I lay there crying. It was California
and the sheep vision. I was on a mattress
looking up. I started to talk. Aside
from the stars, aside from the beating heart, I only
remember two things: both hands were in the air
and I was, for the first time in twenty years,

lying down without fear. My friend Robin
was there beside me; she was sobbing; I have
such gratitude toward her. It was her house,
it was her stars. She took me down to see

the sheep first, then she showed me the ocean.
It was an outside room; one wall was a maple,
one wall was made of planter boxes. There were

tomatoes and eggplants in one, there was lavender
and basil in another. I remember
the trees on every side; I know there was oak
and redwood; there was a twisted madrona with leaves
in leathery piles, almost like rhododendron.
Robin knew the shadows, she knew the edges,
she knew the clouds, she knew the sky. It was

the summer of 1989. The charts
have already registered my odd affliction
and the stars absorbed my happiness. Standing—
or lying—you could see a horse to the right,
if you were facing north, and a white dragon,
if you were facing south. I think I never
slept that night. I only dozed. And ranted.

Two Daws

for Stanley Kunitz

The false dawn in Wheeling, West Virginia
is five o'clock—given the season—given
the inclination of two or three daws to sing
outside my frozen room; there is some fog,
there is some light; the birds go back to sleep
then, something like I do, waking themselves I'm sure
just as I do with something of a snort
when finicky memory combines with green sulphur—
in their case maybe it's vile hunger combining
with cold, slightly different. I call it "false" dawn
as if it were a fixture; I will talk
to two or three others, a sweet librarian,
a morose poet; I always check to see
if there is a cosmos to match my own. I learned
thirty years ago how odd my thoughts were,
how I could not be trusted. If *I* described
the morning I would say there are two dawns,
one, if it's late April, if it's in the East,
it's night still, there is a kind of thin blue
over the hills; and, two, the true dawn, then
the trees are almost shaking with noise, the sun
is spread out, light is everywhere. There are
two deaths as well—though I will have to check it—
false death, there is a bird then, still a daw,
or sometimes a jay, depending on the season,
and the location; I think in West Virginia
it could be any of twenty birds, the cardinal
is good, the dove is good, they sing with such a

note—such notes—of pity my nose is red
from weeping, my eyes are swollen, there are creases
of woe in my forehead, I am dragging my feet
like never before, it is a sacrifice
and I am holding the knife; I want it to be
a stone knife—I can pick my weapon. The other
the birds are silent; I would have them screaming
and scolding, but I have no authority there.
Kunitz, may he live forever, says
there's only one dawn. It's like an orchestra,
first, say, a lark, or first a robin, and then
it's the finch's turn; maybe the flutes are first
and then the cellos and the flutes are silent.
That is the lull. We in the trombones slide
slowly, don't we—what a din we made.
But there are *two* deaths, he's wrong—only once—that gorgeous
poet, there are *two* deaths, though now I remember
he only spoke of "dawn," he didn't speak
of "death"—he never said there weren't two deaths—
I was the one who brought up those birds and had them
singing and scratching twice, he kept his counsel
on death, and everyone I talked to we reasoned
together about two "dawns," and almost everyone
said there were two, or they agreed with me
to show how smart they were or they just found
the thought intriguing. No one said there were,
or said there weren't, two deaths; I'm all alone
with my two deaths, I have to make my own birds

and my own cat, for that matter, sitting and watching
or walking slowly by with a flea collar
choking him, or dragging a bell from his throat.
—False dawn maybe is only a light birds are
fooled by, though the light could be from within,
triggered by fear—or hunger; I almost think it's
curiosity—which kills all birds. False death
is almost like it; light from something drags us
out, breathing our last, fresh blood pumping
through our necks and wrists, terror forcing us
down, last-minute cunning, last-minute hope
saving us—counting to ten, humming, laughing,
at what I called light—instead of darkness—knowing
more than I say—more than I can say—but true dawn—
ah sapsuckers singing from my birch, the branches
of my giant arbor vitae shaking, the needles
of my great yews dancing, not to mention the copper
beach, or the weeping willow, not to mention
the crab apple, not to mention the dying
redbud, not to mention the oak. The word
"dawn" it comes from "daw," there has to be
some connection with the bird; "daw"
is middle English: "there are two daws"; "death"
is from old Frisian, that from old Saxon, that from
old High German. When it comes to true death
Kunitz is just like me, I guess, polite
and a little terrified, certainly amazed. I
have nothing to say about which birds; I think

of crows, naturally, although that should be false
death, shouldn't it? I say that with respect
for one soul and another. I think it's geese
I think about, walking with their webbed feet
down some greasy path, honking with caution,
almost with rudeness, yet lifting their huge bodies
and disappearing, in ten or twelve seconds, life
and death are in their rising and falling; swallows
are birds of death, in and out, trees
I won't get started on, either here, wherever
here is, or in the next place, or in the last place,
not one locust, not one cyprus. I
am full of spring these days, I listen to a hundred
sounds of shrieking every morning. Kunitz
is right about the orchestra—and yet,
isn't it reversed? Isn't true dawn
the one that is operatic? Shouldn't I sing then,
breathing my last, fretting over my own death
among the other birds? And shouldn't I sleep
like a wise man through the false dawn even if the first
thin blue is out there, even if there is a call
from one or two creatures, even if the cardinal
is making me moan, and even if the chickadee
is hanging upside down and banging his head
against the shiny glass—even if the worm
is fighting for his life and the lily of the valley
is bowing her head in shame, shouldn't I live on?

3

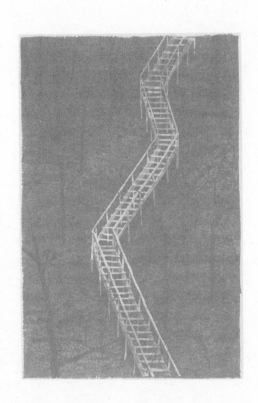

Her Right Eye Catches the Lavender

for Judy Rock

What is the eastern gull called? Is it the same one
that floats in the Iowa River? I read in *Birds*
it has pink legs—yellow eyelids in summer.
Why did I never see that? Can I drive
a thousand miles to live among them, watch
them hop and lift their wings a little, see them
fold their legs back as they soar? Someone

named Rock was walking by the water; she threw
salami at them. Knowing her as I do
I know she chose one of them and pursued him
relentlessly—her eye is part of her mind—
and though there would be patter she never would lose him
until he was gone. I don't know how she feels
about them as scavengers, I don't know if she
calls them rats with wings or if she finds them
endearing, as I do, with their gorged bodies
and drooping wings—gobbling doves—if she
forgives them, as I do, for their gluttony,
if she watches them fighting the currents, if she compares them
to hawks, if she compares them to pigeons. After

her walk on the beach she lay down with her clothes on
in one of those shingled houses, on starched sheets
with eyelets at the borders, maybe flowers—
faded peas or roses. There was a roomful
of crisp white linen, there was a pear-shaped bottle
with three carnations, there was a wedding bouquet

with ivory streamers—curled up on the bureau—
and there was a drawing of Thomas Hardy's birthplace
in Dorset, and a painting above the bed
of an apple orchard in bloom, it was cloudy
and humming. She woke up at six and watched
the light get stronger in the windows, the one
a lemon pink, the other a pearl gray,
both of them filled with branches, and she thought
a little about her happiness. Day and night

the gulls eat, although they rest; they fall
asleep in a second. Even if there is some shifting,
even gurgling, they are asleep. It is
sleep that alters their rage, sleep slows down
their appetites, it is their only substitute
for pity—even as it renews
their life of greed. I think she must get up,
I think she smiles; she rummages through her suitcase
looking for something, she kneels at the foot of the bed
with one hand under her chin; her right eye catches
the lavender. I have her letter, I am
more voracious than I was seven years ago
but I am more lenient. I watch them catch the wind,
then race downstream. Why did it take so long
for me to get lenient? What does it mean one life
only? Could I not stand in the mud
beside my black willow, thinking of her and loving her?

Those Things

With one foot on the standpipe
I bend down to tie my soaking shoe
 a block from everything,
the Back Stage Deli, the Roosevelt Hotel,
 the French consulate.
I walk up Vanderbilt, across Forty-seventh
 under the canopy
of Maggie's Place, into the Paris Croissant.
 I am on the East Side
for the first time in years, in an East Side drizzle,
 pushing against umbrellas,
walking through taxicabs, touching wet dogs.
 Someone else
is going to smoke a cigarette, someone
 is going to stumble through
the olives and fettucini and spinach with some kind
 of hope—or terror—I
will put my arm on the table, I will talk
 to Tintoretto, I will smear
catawba blossoms on my cheeks, I will
 argue with Amos, I
will walk away with my head in my hands, Dio-
 nysus again, the veins still struggling,
the heart still pumping away. I have to retreat
 to West Virginia, to North Carolina,
my city in southern Mexico, my mountain
 in northern Greece. A man
has two dark stages in his life; the first

he puts *those things* to the side;
he comes upon them lifting a stone, or turning
     a corner, something touches him,
he moans, he moans in his sleep, he turns the other
     corner, he is besieged a little,
his hair, his hair turns white, he combs it out
     of his brush, the terror of dying,
the body turned around—that is his sign;
     the second stage is later, he is
 freed a little, bored a little, but still
     he is filled with passion—what
would you call it otherwise?—He leaves New York,
     he leaves the Paris Croissant, the Louvre
is pasted on the wall, the glass pyramid
     is on the other side, the solstice
is not for him, endless light, ridiculous
     chanting, he needs another table,
a cave this time, maybe that bench at last
     outside his library, every word
scorched this time, this time he listens, this time
     he has forever. What will he wear?
he thinks. What will he read? What will he drink?
     And what will he do for love this time?
For love will he bend down like a crow? Will he listen?
     Will he write three dozen letters? He
is sitting again, his hand is holding a pencil,
     and he is drinking. He has picked
a flower from a battlement, the lily

of Spain it's called—in France it is
a weed and grows between the stones, it is
        his flower, he puts it in a glass,
he puts it in his pocket, it is better
        than a death's-head, some poor creature on
his table, a thumb in her mouth, the Bible lying
        open, a candle making shadows—
love, not death, for him to think about,
        a flower, such a pretty thing,
another year of life it means, it means
        that he will have to wait a little,
that he will live on his stomach dreaming, that he
        will turn the petals to the light,
that he will have yearning again, and greed, and sorrow.

His Song of the Green Willow

I guide my darling under the willow tree
to increase the flow of her blood.

A branch weeps, so does she, a twig breaks off
like one of her thoughts.

We are helpless together, we spend the night
listening to shameless sounds

and study the moon together, watching it spread
knowledge over the white mulberry.

Whoever lies down first, that one will hear
the cardinal first, and that one will see the streaks

above the lilacs. Whoever does not leave,
whoever is loyal, whoever stays, that one will see

the rabbits thinking, that one will see a nest
and small ones warm from living. Whoever sits up

and looks at the sky—whoever is alone—
that one will be the griever, that one will make

his song out of nothing, that one will lean on his side
and stir the ground with his stick—and break his stick—

if that is his way, and moan, if that is his way,
and go on forever—his thirty-two feet at a time—

thirty-two feet until the branches start
and the scattered twigs,

her thoughts again—for him her thoughts—his song
of the green willow, her song of pain and severance.

it is better to cut a hole yourself
and let the gum well up. The cry of justice
is greater than any other cry; all things
begin and end with that cry. What do you think the
scales are? What do you think is balanced? Ah, he
kicks at the cat; he runs into a garbage can,
he certainly slides in the mud; he certainly loses
his glasses, *that* is justice. What he does
he does in twenty square feet, between a birch
and an arbor vitae, what he does he does
with so much knowledge that he can forgive himself
for anything. One of his hands, he thinks,
stands for one thing and one of them stands for another.
He needs them both to hold up the birch. He favors
one and so he pushes the other, even
here there has to be justice, there has to be
consideration. He turns to the barberry, he picks
two berries, he has learned to watch out for thorns—
and if the lark had thorns, if it had a stench,
if it could screech—he's seen his orange cat cower
a dozen times, she runs from shadows. Sometimes
he leans against the trunk, sometimes he stretches
his shortened hamstrings; he loves a certain twilight—
that first darkness doesn't depress him—sometimes
he holds the lowest branch, for him it is
a restful position, sometimes he pulls at the bark
and reads the yellow page, sometimes he chews
on one flamboyant leaf, sometimes on another.

The Smell of Death

Green fishes swimming in the street
and white clematis climbing a wooden fence
for our last walk together.

A rose with such an odor
that to bend down and smell it
is to live again like two Babylonians,
one with her hair so heavy that when she bends over
she holds it with two hands,
one with his beard so thick and curly
that when he bends over
his chest, where the linen falls, is cool
as the ground was where the dead leaves lay.

A mulberry tree—two mulberry trees—two babies
so thin that they are thinner than weeds the doves
planted there overnight, the doves who ate
a mile away from here and flew here with food
filling their stomachs, rich and sticky food.

And two hibiscus blossoms faced two ways
on the same stem,
like trumpets, or like ears to gather in
the sounds of our grieving—

Two paper heads, I should say, two round heads
with plaited cheeks and seedy noses that have
an inch of wisdom between them,

heads that they fold at night and keep half-folded
for days on end
like wilted cabbage leaves, like thick handkerchiefs,
folded to keep the cold out—is that it?—like two
white heads on the same pillow, like two flat heads
faced eye to eye, if there were eyes, and even
mind to mind, if there were minds; for me

there are only hearts—like two red hearts then
somewhere inside those roots, unless the flowers
themselves are what they call hearts, two flowers, then, talking
for the last time, they could be from a single
bud for all I know, two brutal flowers
turning away from each other, spending their last night
plotting and thinking, barely closing, concentrating
on their own bitterness, hating, for all I know,
the concrete borders and the broomfuls of dirt,
hating the sun, for all I know, one of them—
I want to say—more bitter, I want to say
more brutal, but what do I know, one of the two
round heads myself; I want to say she is hateful
of light itself. I think, to my embarrassment,

of a flattened squirrel, a kind of glove, her mouth
more simpering every day, I think of cone flowers
lying in my garbage, a layer of plaster,
then a layer of flowers; I think of the heads

buried in glass, the pointed heads, the stalks
foolish in that position. The fishes are seedpods

that cover the street for a day or two—some tree
or other—why should I think *that* strange? My seed
would have filled three buckets—isn't that lovely?
It goes with the putrid squirrel. I stop to smell
the smell of death, I kick it a little, fumes
rise, there is a god that loves it, he smacks
his lips, like a dog; the smell of death, we say,
a catch in our voice: I smelled it once in the Bronx

walking back to the subway; there was a corpse
lying behind some bushes, I was there
for the People's Convention, Reagan came, and Carter,
they promised to rebuild the Bronx—I think the corpse
was holding his nose—he had to be either Black
or Puerto Rican; some girls, as if to test me,
as if to see if I could be shocked, guided me
back to the body; I think he had been there for three
whole days, in the heat of July; all of the buildings
were empty; that was 1980; we had

two summers, didn't we, my darling. I think of that,
my round head on the pillows. I use four now,
like a duchess, darling, flowers, stripes and always
a heavy white; I lie on my stomach sometimes

to rest my neck, I make room for my nose
by turning a fraction to the right, I free
one of my ears so I can hear the fan
mix with the music. There is one pillowcase

I love more than the others; I hunt for that one
most of the time; I think it was pale blue once
but it is almost white from so much washing,
the way the sky was after it rained; I saw that
in my part of the garden with my huge
red eye an inch or two away from you
with your red eye, and your paper head, my sweet,
trying to follow my words as I had to strain
with yours—I always had to—a foot away
from the sullen lupines and the ruthless lilies, my darling.

Red with Pink

It is a great weariness, isn't it,
almost a kind of sorrow,
getting up before you're ready
because of a babbling in the maples.
It is a great bitterness, pressing
one ear at a time to the ground
beside the green delphiniums,
calling up the worms, cocking
your own bird head, walking through
the chives, picking one or two clouds,
putting them in a crushed vase,
certainly a sadness, touching
the trunk of a dead dogwood
where a thick vine choked it
yet left an elegant imprint
as if a snake had lain there
waiting for the babbling to stop.
    My hand is in that tree,
or maybe only three fingers,
it is so narrow; I can't
be buried inside, there is
no room for my legs, I need
a cherry or a sycamore.
I break a branch off, a twig
instead of a branch, a stem—
if that is smaller—I water
the lupines, they are almost shameful,
I water the white bleeding hearts,

I turn the earth into mud,
I lift a blossom to my face,
I let one drop or two
fall on my table; I save them
for later. If I look
at the two sides of the flower
a green wedge is driven
through the middle; that is—
though I don't want to say it—a heart
broken in two; the drop
is a kind of platform, it springs
the blossom open; white drops
are everywhere, and pollen,
a kind of semen, though in this case
love had to be reversed.
      I wrap my thumb and finger
around the dogwood; that is
a way of remembering, probably
a way of thinking; even
a cane wouldn't be this thin;
there never was substance, it never
was truly a tree. Ten feet
away, as the red ant crawls—
if that—the orange roses
are snarled in honeysuckle;
that is a way of crying
in two languages at once,
Polish and Yiddish, medieval

Greek and Irish; one voice
holds up the other. We say
they cry, but they rage, they choke
on their beauty, they die in their bloom.
I say they "die" but one of them
lives, even if it is crippled.
I tried to disengage
the one from the other; I ripped
out leaves from my wire fence—
long live honeysuckle, it sticks
to wire—long live orange roses,
they came there first. Ten feet
away another rose bush
is growing; this one is free
of honeysuckle, though it is
more like a shrub, it falls
apart when you touch it, that is
a kind of freedom, isn't it,
living unsnarled, no sweetest
of sweets to hold you, falling
apart at the touch; I lived
in New York like that, falling
apart at the touch; I walked
up Avenue C or First Avenue,
I gave up ever seeing again
the bluejay under my birch,
the wind driving him crazy;
I gave up chives, and poppies,

and lived in a white shirt, walking
and running by turns—oh sweetest
of sweets, I disentangled
myself from the honeysuckle,
I loosened the morning glory,
I gave up the choking feeling
east on Fourth Street, north
on Second, past the Bangladesh
laundry, past the white gunny sacks
of rice. I had to be a rose
one more time. I had to be
open and airy. I stopped
in a Polish restaurant. I first went
down three steps to the entrance—
a rose going down three steps
is quite a sight, and a rose
eating his soup, even on
First Avenue next to McDonald's
on one side and something Spanish
on the other is rare, and a rose
learning Greek so he could
talk to his neighbor from Samos
is also rare. I could have
studied Polish, or Ukrainian,
but that is not decent for this kind
of rose, whether red or yellow,
whether ivory tinged with salmon

or orange with a crimson base
or blue with pink.
                    I learned
her name while basking on a wall—
Vassilia—it is the Greek
for "royal"; if she were a rose
she would be lilac with a white edge
and when the wind blew her down
she would be more white than blue,
a modern color combining
old thoughts. I know we first met
outside the Temple to Hera
a half a century ago
when she was eighteen and I was
a few years younger. I tell her
this in English, we are sitting
with the wire fence between us
in our own courtyards an hour
from New York City. I tell her
how much I loved Samos; she smiles
when I name her village; our roses
are almost alike, they come
from the same green sticks; she sits
with shears in her hand; I sit
with a pencil in mine; her stockings
are rolled; she almost knows
my name. Her husband is blind,

he is in Samos; my wife
lives in New York. She was
pink with brown edges; she was
very dark red. I live
by myself now. I am scattered.

Someone Will Do It for Me

If that dove leaves before I do
I will have the wall to myself
and the onion sets and the wooden tulips.
I alone will swing my legs
and flap madly over the telephone wire
and through the dead maple.
I have no trouble with this
or with shrieking, when it comes,
or even with gobbling from a sunken pan
or a glass or dirty water.
I understand how, for one day,
I have the body of another,
be he a fat and nimble handyman
or she a spindle-legged half-blind hydroptic.
I carry it from one wet roof to another
and I return constantly to a certain canyon
and a certain cement sidewalk.
Poor things whose fate
is with a small-headed bird
with ruined eyes
and a way of dragging himself as if he were made of mud.
No responsibility on this end,
avoiding red bricks, paying attention to diet;
they will have to stay with me
and trust I'll live and live,
sleeping in the gutters, burying my head
under my bloodless wing.
And what about me—what bird of mine?

Where could he be? Will I slide
down the roof as gently as a man
going in for supper? Will I choke
on tongue again and this time swallow the rind
or this time when a bullet
hits my chin first, then my soft neck,
will I bleed to death just off route 24
with no one there to scream,
or will I be in my T-shirt
brushing one tooth at a time
smiling again in the cracked mirror;
or sweeping the piece of concrete
between the brick wall and the wire fence
with special gestures for the cherry stones
and the red leaves? Poor white one,
you will have to learn it all, the rashness,
the wandering, the secrecy, as I am learning the name
of the Greek next door, sitting in his tomatoes,
reading his paper; as I am planting an iris
only for him, among the hollyhocks,
as I am smiling at him, as I am writing
his name—Augoustis Bozakis—in my tablet
and the name of his wife—Vassilia—and the island
she comes from. Someone will do it for me, someone
will see me with my legs crossed and my pencil
going back and forth, he'll watch me with my orange
against the wall, looking into the sunshine,
and write my name down just as it would have been

if we had stayed in Kiev, if there had not been
one separation after another; he'll know
my American name and my embarrassment.
I wish I could see the tablet. What is it called
seeing yourself that way? Is it a final
understanding, or is it just shabby pity
and shabby revenge? There are doves colliding
in both skies; there is such interchange
it is almost frenzy, such hijinks—
heavy landing and puffing and bitter warbling—
it is almost relief.

I Would Call It Derangement

I cut a stick for my love. It is too early
to clear the yard. I pick some lilac. I hate them
dying on the vine. I plan my assault
on the dead maple. I will tie some rope
to the rotting side and pull it down so I can
cut it limb from limb without destroying
the phone connections from one state to another
or smashing the new tomato plants and ruining
the asters. She is walking from place to place
and wrapping herself in sheets. If the wind
were free up there it would lift the curtains
just as it bends the poppies and the yearning
iris. I am setting a table. I
am smiling at the Greeks next door. I put
an old gardenia in the center, something
that has some odor. We are in the flowery
state now. I spill half the petals over
her watermelon; only here are flowers
good for eating, here and India
where they are sprinkled over colored ice
and onto the half-cooked fish. I have a system
for counting bricks but this one day I study
the clouds that move from left to right and the swallows
hunting for food. They seem to fly in threes
and alternately flap their wings, then skim
the roofs; they even make a sound, some brief
chipping; I hear it when they come in range,
maybe when they fight for space. One cloud

is black, it goes from a simple skeleton
to a bloated continent. Given my inclination,
I will turn it into a blowfish before
breakfast is over—or an uprooted tree.
Upstairs she sings—she chips—I know she's dancing
with something or other. When she comes down she'll have
the static of the radio on her tongue,
she understands the *words*, she actually sings
those songs—her voice is a high soprano—I
love it going up and down. My voice is ruined
but I can do a kind of quaver. I have
unearthed the wisdom from my second decade,
and though it did the world little good and even
served as a backdrop to our horrors I don't
blame the music, I can't blame the music
if the horrors grow stronger every year.
She listens to me with one hand, eating sugary
pineapple with the other. I listen too,
under the washrag and the dead maple,
hearing the words for the first time, making her scream
with laughter at my words, almost lucid
compared to hers, as hers are labyrinthian
compared to mine. There is this much music
in eastern Pennsylvania and this much love
and this much decadence. I would call it
derangement—the swallows twice a day
have it, and the white delphiniums
turning to blue again and the orange snapdragons.

If we could lie down for a minute we would let
the bastardy of our two decades take over
just as we let the songs do; there is nothing
that doesn't belong with love; we can't help it
if anguish enters; even leaving the world
as we do there is no disgrace, that is
another kind of anguish—just as it was
following a band of swallows, just as it was
bending down to taste the flowers or turning
the clouds into overturned trees or smiling in Greek.

The Thought of Heaven

There is one blossom on my redwood table
I smell for hours, even holding it
like a handkerchief in the palm of my hand
and bringing it to my face. I recognize it
as a kind of thought, as in the black locust
the poor of the world for one or two weeks a year
have their paradise, nor is it disgraceful
nor is it weak and seedy even if the thorns
make their wrists bleed, even if the leaves
they love to strip are dry; as in the phlox,
the weightless phlox, the bees drag down, the six
colors of lavender, a field of wild ninnies
growing like grass where there is a little room
beside the road; as in the bridal wreath
that smells like honey, that covers a city with cream,
there is one day for pomp; as in the dogwood
there is one day for sadness, four curled petals
with drops of blood, growing white or pink
in the cold dirt, all the more to be
the contrast, under some maple or huge cherry,
for me a blossom of thought supreme, nothing
in the world like it; as in the colored weeds
on my dashboard; as in the flowers in all five pockets;
as in my blue jacket once I found twenty years
of thought—more than that—the election
of Lyndon Johnson, the death of Eleanor Roosevelt—
look how they are political—Americans
in Lebanon, in Hispaniola; I sit there

like a tailor, cleaning out lint, whatever
lint is, holding a stem in the air, rubbing
a golden flower through my fingers, catching
the spots of light. The sun is on my left,
the poppies are in my driveway, a wild exchange
is taking place in my yard, something between
my dwarf apples; yellow dust is falling
into the sweet-smelling glue—this is thought,
even if it's copulation, it is a tried
and true intrigue, an old flirtation; there are
swollen stamens and green lipstick; Plato
would be the first to forgive me, but I don't think
of forgiveness now these last few decades. I
struggle past my willow; someone has cursed me
with a weeping willow, it is Chinese and grows
in swamps best, that I remember, swamps and bogs,
that and the sycamore; if anything,
I'll turn away; if anything I'll sit
among the broken sticks facing the fenced-in
weeds, revenge on ground hogs; I will stare
for a minute or two at a private flower, that is
enough for one day—who is it wants to sit
forever anyhow? There are two months
left—I should say three—the wind and the sun
will help me, so will water, so will bees,
for all I know, and moths, and birds; ah what
dark thoughts once rested in our coats, all of us,
dogs and cats and humans, not only burrs,

not only prickles; how it scatters first
and then floats back; that is what they called
a germ; it was Hegelian; I have
to find the pre-Socratic, that is for me
what thought should be, I am a sucker still
for all of it to hang together, I want
one bundle still. When the sweet scent comes from the east,
though I call it a thought, it is, as it should be,
something that precedes thought—that is a way
of putting it—something that accompanies thought,
but it is *thought* as it drifts down over the Chinese
willow, as it floats above the table
and penetrates my doors and windows; I bow
down to it, I let it change me, that
is the purpose of thought—I call it all thought, whatever
changes you. Dear apple, I am ready.
What is it for you, is it dreaming, does that set you
free? I call a bursting "dreaming," I call
a rage and sundering by its sweet-smelling name,
as if I were a child domesticating
everything within a mile for purposes
of my own rage. There is a thought. It is
if not in this blossom then in another, in
the lilies of our highways, in the great
round thistles beside them, in the black-eyed susan,
the flower I always bend down for, most of all—
for two or three weeks at least—in the chicory,
blue with the dust of the universe, a blue

more like lavender—I would call it purple
if I were extreme—I would say the edges
are white from gripping the sky, or they are drained
from so much thought. I call it the thought of heaven,
not too disgraceful for the chicory,
solemn and blue as it is, such is my thinking.

4

Bread Without Sugar

In memory of Harry Stern, 1897–1969

This is what makes justice in the world—
to bring these lives into the light.
　　　　　　　　　—Grace Paley

The first time I saw the stone
I was overjoyed that I would be
keeping him like that. I cried
at the back of my mouth—a kind of gasp,
a kind of sucking in of air,
more in the way of surprise, maybe
terror even—though I was at peace,
even though I covered my mouth
as if I were still coming out of the garden
the way it was when we were boys
together. I never put a shawl
over my lower face; it was
the delicate fingers over my lips
in front of the Rosenberg rat-strewn bakery:
my mouth was open—I stood for a while
somewhere between two continents, somewhere
on an overnight flight. I should have been freezing
in New York City or Chicago; there was
saltwater down there, there was sand
and shallow roots. I should have been standing
or kneeling a little, one knee wet—
or dirty; it was December. I long for
that staggered wall again, for the street light
that makes the garbage glow. I long for
the Plumbing and Heating sign, my own
plastic basket reflected in the glass,

a Gauguin sky, an airplane floating
through the window of a skyscraper.
And I should have sat on my haunches holding
a bowl of rice to my lips, half lost
in thought the way a Chinese teacher,
a poet, would also be lost—say one
from Hunan Province—looking over
the empty lot, the windswept garbage,
a hundred wires holding him together,
pulley and phone and electric.

                               I stood
facing a row of mean-hearted elders
who made money in the 1960s
from a sudden flutter in the stock market,
tough little boys who learned to read
the newspapers and move the columns
of wooden and metal beads. They read
the *Miami Herald*—it was two inches
thick—cars and furniture and cruises
dripped all over their rugs. I slipped
on the television buy of the century once;
I fell down on a velour sofa—
it was either a kitchen banquette
or the backseat of a Chrysler New Yorker.
The *Herald* is thicker than the *Dispatch*,
thicker than the *Star-Ledger*,
thicker than the *Post-Gazette*.

There wives are beside them. Did I think
they'd meet on the sly and pull out names
and numbers forever? Did I think
they'd whistle a little and talk about streets
in Flatbush and Newark, and talk about houses,
how solidly they were built, some restaurant
they always stood in front of? It
was the same restaurant in Newark and Flatbush,
there was a blonde at the cash register,
she was beautiful in the style
of 1941. They ate
fruit salad sundaes—the fruit was tasteless
but pretty, the syrup was heavy—the war
was on their lips: there was one battle
south of Naples and there was another
on a tiny Asian atoll; the bodies
were cut to ribbons on the coral;
there would be Japanese hidden there
for thirty years to come. Their lives
in Newark and Flatbush would always be hooked,
they would always be crisscrossed with someone
showing up at a wedding, or leaning
inside a window while a family
was eating supper, a look of meekness—
futility—on his face, his hair
unbecomingly long, exhaustion,
grief, and curiosity taking over,
the war neither won nor lost.

                                    My mother
walks like a sparrow; I love her at last
without vexation. I am reckless
the way I was when I was twelve,
maybe fourteen, before I broke loose,
before I started to build a cave
inside my throat, before I claimed
only stricken things to the dismay and anger—
even the admiration sometimes—
of my young parents, starched sparrows
worrying over the pockmarked bread
that looked so much like limestone, that tasted
so bland without sugar—bread without sugar,
we ate it daily. Would you believe
my food if I told you? Would you not gasp
and roll your eyes? Milk was the poison
I ate before my meat—that was
the way we did it, that was how
we pleased the Levites; how would they know
the meat wasn't already boiling in milk
once it was in my stomach? She is
more like pigeon, my mother: she hobbles,
although I thought of her, almost in her nineties,
as some small bird; the wind must take her,
she is like wild grass, she lunges
from place to place, she runs; I lift her
into the buses, I hold her down
as if she were paper. This is the pain

I stayed away from, I could just bear
the endless separation better,
the cruelty of one short phone call
a week; but I am reckless, I sing
some Edith Piaf for her, she loves
the culture between the wars, she knows
the French—we school each other; I make her
breakfast before we leave, we take
a cab, there is such sighing, I pay him
to drive us into the cemetery;
I want to see how it looks with trees
growing beside the walks; I want
to see some shadows. Oh God, in Pittsburgh
the Russian graveyard was on three hills;
the paths were narrow and twisted; it took
an hour to find someone; and there was
such a shortage of space you found
the souls on top of each other, the head
of one stone facing the foot of another
the way it was in our bedrooms in
the first brick house, the ferns half-soaring
above our faces. But in this swamp
there is such space that they can build
a city for the dead that stretches
for thirty miles if they have to: the Jews
of Bucharest, the Jews of Berlin,
the Jews of Paris with white napkins tugging
at their throats, the Jews of Lima

already looking like Indians, the Jews
of Leningrad with music in their hands,
and the Jews of Detroit and the Jews of Toronto
speaking Spanish again, going back
to the fifteenth century, bowing and lisping,
learning it, bitterly now, from the Cubans,
taking their places with the Nicaraguans
and Venezuelans, remembering words
they hadn't thought of for five hundred years—
the names for dessert, the names for love,
the names for bitter wind, and the names
for silence: there are so many good names
for that—nor was it ever lost,
in one warm place and another, the streets
going down to the water, sailors and thinkers
always with trunks on their backs, a secret
message sewn somewhere, something explained
to their joy, something overlooked to their sorrow.

There are two plots, the third is in France,
the third is in Egypt; I go from country
to country in search of a plot; I see me
buried in Poland—what a nightmare *that* is!—
I go to see my mother's city
and on the second day while waiting
for Gregor Musial, my Polish translator,
I am hit by a cab; I'll never
die of a heart attack in Warsaw,

and known the cheap cut; his feeling
e showed in how he touched
. I wanted to sit and talk
all my life—I wanted to have
ether, but he couldn't be
h me, something drove him
he was only happy
dforsaken—and children. He died
ance—an error—but he
a word to the squad; I am
of him, I am violent;
m, but he was so mild
nplained, that Aaron.

                    The sky
night; I love the tropics,
nderneath the blue; green parrots
t of the sun, voices
t of the ground, it must be
Sosna, these are his neighbors,
d Katz; some are New Yorkers,
Cincinnati, one
Africa, one is from Turkey—
w grapefruit. When they sing
in the movies or they
y were sitting down there
ark, on Wednesday afternoon.
our downfall, schmaltz was our horror,

I'll never catch pneumonia, not there;
the cab will lose its steering and jump
the curb; of course I'll be the one sitting
closest to the street, I'll be reading
the newspaper with a dictionary,
I'll be reading the principal poets
in Polish and English; the cabbie can't give
a day up to find the part, maybe have
his cousin make one in his garage—
there are no spare parts in Poland. What a
fate for a Jew from Pittsburgh, guilt
and sadness driving him for fifty years,
to join his brothers and sisters that way,
blood spreading over his cotton shirt,
a circle of Polacks around him, a cop
going through his wallet, scratching his neck
with his metal nightstick. What does it matter?
Where should my site be? In Texas? Arizona?
I am more scattered than my father was,
born in Kiev, died in Miami.
There is the crow—I thought I'd wait
for hours for him. There is the gull.
There is a robin—from Pennsylvania—
I know him by his hop, I know him by his stance,
he and a worm are struggling together,
the robin's legs are spread. The stone
is gray—and streaked—the letters are deep;
Vermont granite. I am left

with stone, my father is made of stone,
he is one of the stones half-walking
in crooked formation, in Opa-Locka;
his place is by the fence, Meyer Schwartz
is behind him, Abe Wagner is his friend—
his neighbor. There is garbage not far
from the grave; it is the people living
on the other side: their cars are there,
their saucers are there, they throw their cardboard
and plastic over the vine-strewn fence.
The cantor is dead who sang at his grave;
the rabbi is dead, the boring rabbi
with the slanting hand; I gave him the money
to split between them; they hated each other,
law and music estranged them. I learned
pity from my father, I learned silence.
I tried to master his grief.

                    I was
forty-four when he died. It was
the worst snowstorm in northern New Jersey
in fifty years—the lines were down;
it took a day to reach me; Newark
and La Guardia were closed; I had to
take a train to Philadelphia
and fly from there. The schools were shut,
the snow was over the windows. I didn't
own a suit. I walked two miles

to Robert Hall—it was the o
store open. A salesman was
inside—he thought I was cr
the cuffs done for me someh
he was a tailor too—it was
a heavy wool suit. I stood fo
on a wooden platform, the
the tracks were covered with
was a local; it ran from Nev
to Philadelphia; we used to
the Pennsylvania railroad; i
my train—I knew every sto
at the Union Station in Pit
wagons, unloading boxcars
the filthiest air in history; t
a yellow cloud hanging ov
and there were cinders—cl
in the grand hall; I loved i
loved the disgusting smell.
had thirty-eight suits, the
were woven together—sor
a buyer, a merchandise ma
and he had fifty wide ties;
a pleasure to see him get
was hot—it was in Februa
it was eighty degrees or n
the suit I wore to the fun
have felt the cloth and kn

was made,
for others
their cloth
with him—
one day to
at peace w
wild. I thi
with the G
in an ambu
couldn't sa
rude becau
I shocked
he never c

is streaked
the orange
are flying
are rising
Yaglom an
and Felder
one is from
was born i
he would k
they do it
do it as if
in Lummu
Schmaltz w

we wept on the streets or walked to the swimming pool
weeping, we drove to the bakery weeping.
What was it for? What did we long for
so much, what had we lost? Was it
so shocking to live here? Did we not live
like angels? Why did we need such pity?
Why was there always such odd vexation?
One voice is heavy, it loves itself
and lingers in *basso profundo*; one voice
is dark, it is the alto I dreamed of,
the sound is like a cello. They sing
about dust, they sing about mouths, they sing
about mercy; they have delicate memories,
although there is no desire for blood—
that is absurd to them; their words
are drumlike, it is the sound of boxes,
the sound of barrels—I know the music.
Do you know Abe Corn? He drove us there
the second day—we couldn't find the footstone
our first visit. He was a cop
in his other life; he came from Vienna;
he was brutal, but he waited like a chauffeur
the whole morning while we probed in the dirt
for the name. My father was the only one there
without a name.

                    This petulant city
is in despair a little: there was

some burning, two blacks were shot for riding
a red motorcycle—the mayor is working
hard to legalize red motorcycles,
though red excites the police. You go
from the graveyard east to 95,
the ocean is on your left—so are
the Azores, so is Carthage, so is
India. What have we done? We don't know
who to ask for forgiveness. Far from
that, we delight in our own slaughter,
but Miami is honest at least: either rust
corrodes the metal or sunlight bleaches
the cloth or water distends the wood.
And where should I go, to the Art Deco
to see how it merges with the Spanish?
Or should I go back to Córdoba and live
with the Moslems again, or this time the Greeks
and speak Ladino? Should I not
find my own sky to stare at, white lights
burning in the water, the salt
making my red nose quiver? Fat chance
for that—fat chance for a village—I have to
go down to Baja somewhere and watch
the pigs rolling in shit and munch on
some hideous sugar wafers; or sit
in a square in the moutains of Samos sighing
over stone and smiling at Germans half
a century and more after the sorrow.

I was in a forest studying Greek
and trying to learn the symbols when the
angel Sammael squeezed onto
my rock—he stank from the sun—and whispered
six secret words—or seven—I forget;
I even forget if it was Yiddish
or Hebrew, and though I flew to Israel
by Olympia and though I ate two suppers
with the Jewish poets and though we cursed
the government and though I felt
at home with Amos and sweet Josea
and hated the same dwarf kings as they did,
I had to go back to my country, so hate me
for that—and I had to start my next wandering,
so hate me for that. I am going to live
in Chinatown now and I'm going to visit
southern France. I may even go to
Crete, that I loved so much, though I want
to live with the Spanish forever. I love
their food and I love their music; I am
not even dead and I am speaking
their language already; I hope their poets
remember me.

         Tomorrow my plane
is leaving, I'll have a thimbleful of coffee
at the jazzy airport before I walk down
the ramps. I have to make a visit

to the Charles Hotel, I have to walk through
the giant lobby and see who is sitting
on the old sofas and play with the birds
and look at the stairway going down like lightning
directly onto the floor and talk to
the woman who runs the desk and see who
is living there now; it looks like a welfare
hotel, it looks like the checks are coming
from some department or other—the porch
is full of children. I have to see
my father and mother at the same hotel
in 1940 or 1941:
we were the first to sleep in our rooms;
the doors were *louvered*; my God, we ate
at a cafeteria—Hoffmans! There was
a girl named Sonny Uncles—that was
her name—we walked underneath the coconuts;
she was the guide. My father had a plan
to move here—there was a job; there are
three steps to the porch; announcements are everywhere;
and there is a piano still, and a fish tank,
and there are ferns and stucco beams
and glass-brick walls and barbaric paintings.
What would it cost for a room—on the ocean?
Where would I eat—on a hot plate? Where
would the honor come from? Who would give
me love, and delight? What would my son
and daughter think of it? Why does shame

always overtake me? Why does destruction?
—And what would I do with my glasses on the sand?
And how would I find my towel? The wind
is blowing two boats, there must be shrimp
and turtle out there. May the turtles escape
the nets! May I find my ocean! May
the salt preserve me! May the black clouds instruct me!

for Ted Solotaroff